Japanese Garden

"Just noticing the world around us is a deeply spiritual path, and Nellie deVries walks there effortlessly in the delightful haiku-like poems of *Japanese Garden*. It is a quiet sanctuary of noticing. Her mastery of *mono no aware*—the art of capturing the beauty of the fleeting moment—is on display in this accessible and inviting volume, or as she writes, 'This is not a gateless gate / yet the way / is always open.'"

—**Robert Hudson**, author of *The Poet and the Fly*

"*Japanese Garden* is a remarkable collection of poems, inspired as much by the poet's intimate and lyrical encounters with the aesthetics of a particular place as by her affinity with the forms and sensibility of traditional Japanese poetry. Deceptively simple, the poems present a master class in what Robert Bly called 'deep image,' where the realms of the physical and spiritual unite. As Nellie deVries implores us: 'Come!' Wonders await."

—**Phillip Sterling**, Professor Emeritus, Ferris State University

"This thoughtful collection has been as carefully tended as the garden that inspired it. Follow the full circle of Nellie's poems, pausing along the path to notice features, themes, and moods that shift with the changing seasons. *Japanese Garden* is a tranquil, reflective book that draws the reader into quiet wonder. It's my joy to recommend it!"

—**Amy Nemecek**, author of *The Language of the Birds and Other Poems*

"Nellie deVries has a deft touch with words and a discerning eye for vivid details. These delightful haiku will heighten a reader's appreciation for what is seen or anticipated when visiting the Japanese Garden at Meijer Gardens in Grand Rapids, Michigan."

—**Patricia Clark**, author of *O Lucky Day*

"The poems in *Japanese Garden* create perfectly nuanced reflections that embrace each season. They travel from spring, when a finch warbles haiku, to winter, when the poet 'kneels to write a word . . . / sees a pebble cradled in the womb of a rock / . . . and [feels] . . . awe.' Throughout her beautifully paced book, Nellie deVries is 'pull[ing] the door closed / against the past.' In doing so, she opens our eyes to the present that is so vibrantly alive in her garden."

—**Linda Nemec Foster**, author of *Bone Country*

Japanese Garden

Four Seasons of Poems

Nellie deVries

RESOURCE *Publications* • Eugene, Oregon

JAPANESE GARDEN
Four Seasons of Poems

Resource Publications
An Imprint of Wipf and Stock Publishers
199 W. 8th Ave., Suite 3
Eugene, OR 97401

www.wipfandstock.com

PAPERBACK ISBN: 979-8-3852-7243-3
HARDCOVER ISBN: 979-8-3852-7244-0
EBOOK ISBN: 979-8-3852-7245-7

VERSION NUMBER 03/20/26

The four seasons kanji were drawn by the author.

Contents

春

Spring

Kuhi

Journey around the pond.
Gather words, images, calm spaces
to carve into stone.

Kousa Dogwood

Tip to tip the petals
form a net and yet
they cannot grasp the bumblebee.

Sky Mirage

Puffs of cottonwood drift
toward their reflection
clouding the water.

lily pads
like artists' palettes
splattered across the pond

a painted turtle brushes through

Misaki Lantern glows
a midnight beacon
for turtles dipped in moonlight.

Turtle Haven

Island pine pruned short
invites the borrowed view beyond the bridge
closer.

Turtle rises
glistening
to sun herself on the granite lounge
of her private key.

Young robin
speckled buff
silently rocks
in the Juneberry tree
knowing
time will ripen the berries
and his breast.

Come!

A wooden boat
tied to the bamboo landing
awaits.

Common field sparrow
harmonizes hues
with dry sedge and beige rushes
but sings a song of gold.

Copper Buddha leans,
earlobes long,
listening to the earth
for elements
of beginning.
Metallic resonance
makes hair curl into constellations of snails.

Resting in the island gazebo,
the heart of the garden,
we hear a raucous splash
but see only the regular rhythm
of rippling rings.

She chased butterflies
till yellow wings soft-landed
on her blue shoulder.

gold midst cedar leaves
the finch warbles his three lines
trills   five   seven   five

Bonsai

At a young and tender age
the trident maple's roots
were wrapped around
a solid rock.
Now old,
it will not let go.

Sakura

Two geese, three goslings
leave the pond's dark waters
to stroll paths of pink blossoms.

Summer

Thunder drums departing clouds,
gravel paths exhale muggy petrichor,
and in the Shia gazebo
cool breezes prickle her drying arms.

Little cypress boat
tethered to the boathouse dock,
for whom do you wait?

The full moon watches
an old man in cypress boat,
faded blue coat with patches,
fishing pole idle,
while his pen catches tanka.

On the gazebo ceiling,
its center a rising sun
of cross-cut pine,
a young spider
counts growth rings.

I hear you, cardinal,
sparrow,
blackbird with red wings.
You too, sunfish,
when you slap your tail
and make rings   rings   rings.

All the dogwood bracts have fallen.
The remaining green berries stretch long necks
toward the pond
watching
for the next marvelous thing
to happen.

The Way of Tea

I turn this bowl, cool in my hands, rough ceramic
with its knob of black glaze, sip the green foam
whipped by the confident hand of Fujisan,
which stirs me to contemplate this
ceremony stretching back five
centuries like thirteen feet
of brocade obi to
the tea master.

I, too, would like to sip tranquility.

Japanese Tea Ceremony
three tankas

I

one brews the matcha
one sips and admires the bowl
one washes dishes
behind the shoji screen while
harmony taps obi drums

II

you handed me sweets
on a folded white kaishi
and all that is left
is the faint pink impression
of a friendship's new blossom

III

you turn your best bowl
with small hands peeking from your
star-strewn kimono
I drink warm foamy matcha
and find there a nebula

To the Mud Dauber Wasp at the Tea Ceremony

Consider it a sign of respect
that I helped shoo you
through the open window

for you did not know
narrow
middles are not the mode

and if you had stayed
we would have wrapped
your thread-thin waist with yards

and yards of ribbon tied
back as a flower
or butterfly bow

straight up and down
like a kokeshi doll
shiny black head and all.

A cluster of maple keys hangs
translucent and blushing
and at the tip of each arrow
a seed coming of age.

Stop Stone

The Master Gardener says
the one who shot-puts tome ishi
into the placid pond
is on a rocky path.

Soon the silt will settle
and water will clear
where waders planted lilies.
No mud, no lotus.

Birds in love
with this paradise
have managed to eat
all the hidden fruit.

On the lonely island
at the heart of this pond,
a rose of Sharon blooms
passion purple,
crimson bleeding from its center.

Arched Bridge

With your railing worn smooth as bone,
brass plates spanning your joints,
will you always brace us
over ruffled waters?

O
brown
marmorated stink bug
crawling over the lip of the lantern
have you
forgotten
something?
Where is your fire
for this fragrant candle?

Entrance Pavilion

Your lintel
is as high as my nose.
I humbly bow to enter,
grasping the black ring
to pull the door closed
against the past.

Autumn

Leaves falling
burnt orange, speckled gold,
brown and bronze.
The gurgling water takes them
farther down
unless they cling to rocks,
a warmer scheme
as less relenting is the stream.

Old ponderosa pine
crossed with bamboo braces
tied with black twine,
are you ready
to shoulder the burden of winter?

Brown, brittle astilbe
wait for first snow
then still they will be.

Shia Round Gazebo
your wooden seat,
more pleasant than
a chill stone one,
invites me to look out.
Even the burning bush
on the far shore
cannot melt the coldness.

Over the North Waterfall
a maple tree remembers
the colors of peaches
and watermelon.

Island shelter
I see you from afar
but cannot visit today
we changed our clocks
to end saving daylight
and sure enough
I ran short of
hours.

Between that burled cumulus
and me
a squirrel nest
sways in the bluster.

Beside the wisteria arbor
swollen rhododendron buds
wait for the ardor of spring.

The sugar maple
tosses leaves like pink frosting
at its feet.
A breeze whisks them
into windrows.

Near the South Landing
a woolly bear
begins to measure
a boulder's granite length
then stops and looks back
as if to note, "Winter
will have an extra chill.
Go find your coat."

In the little boat,
three yellow leaves
two apples
one puddle of rainwater
wait to be ferried into fall.

South Waterfall

A boulder's fierce snout
and mane of moss
are tamed by years
of tumbling water.

A fence of bamboo splints
arched and tied like wired bonsai
trains us to follow the true path.

Little boat,
in your rain puddle
I see leaves and clouds
and reflections of your past,
a mighty cypress
reaching for the sky.

Mink slinks across the path,
round ears alert
in the yellowed hostas.
"What do you think?"
she asks. "Is my brown coat
sleek enough
for the coming season?"

Winter

Entrance Waterfall

Niwaki curls a treble clef
above the stream
unfurling scales
for the soughing pines.

Above a gray scarf-cloud
a lone airplane
winks its red eye.

Footprints in the snow
prove that visitors still enjoy
a winter day walk
and critters a night
of foraging.

Enlightened

Are you still here, Buddha?
Now there's some white
in your curls.

Empty Boathouse

Pine sprigs and bamboo stalks
secured to the boathouse posts
welcome the New Year.

Solstice

She kneels to write a word by the light of a small lantern,
sees a pebble cradled in the womb of a rock.
Tomorrow, the Gardener will see
knee prints in the snow
and know that someone
knelt in awe.

With solitude a boulder at my back,
I look up.
Orion!
The Hunter has found me.

Even from the hilltop
the teahouse is unreachable.
The Big Dipper tips me a drink
of starlight.

It’s a short hop
to reach the island,
the rabbit’s favorite spot
for winter rumination.

At the gazebo
rhododendron leaves,
river birch branches,
and dried hydrangea blossoms
lead their blue shadows in dance
across glistening snow and flagstone patio.

Tome ishi near the dry fountain
did not slow the deer,
the pebbles tattle.

Hushed Pulse

South Waterfall roars dark
through the moonless evening
rippling the black pond.

Beyond the small island,
snow on ice
glimmers light.

Frogs and fish have found
a deep place
to still their hearts and wait.

Misaki Lantern,
if I could skate to you
and start a warm fire in your heart,
would you lead me to tea?

I try to count the stump's rings
but sit on it instead.
Another year has passed.
I number its beauties.

Buddha,
stick out your tongue
like this
and taste Michigan's winter.

Boathouse Walk

I

Snowmelt drips
from the boathouse eaves,
plipping to echo
the chipping sparrow.

II

An oak leaf
harvesting sun's warmth
melts its handprint in ice.

III

Beside the zigzag boardwalk
pussy willows have opened
soft as a rabbit kit's ear.

West side of the pond in shadows.
Tea house windows shuttered.
A cold cup.

West Gate

This is not a gateless gate
yet the way
is always open.

Your Turn

Now close your eyes
and think of that boat.
Where does it go?
To whom does it float?

Who's in the boat?
Who sits on that seat?
And what do they do
with their hands and their feet?

Is the sun shining
spring-warm, summer-bright?
Or maybe it's foggy.
Maybe it's night.

Is the moon beaming
a silver path as you go?
And what's in the water
and mud down below?

It's your turn to tell,
either here or at home,
what you saw, what you think.
Gather words, write a poem.

Glossary

bonsai	a potted plant
haiku	a short form of Japanese poetry in three phrases following the syllable count 5-7-5
kaishi	a paper folded inside the front of a kimono to be used as a handkerchief, a plate to eat sweets, or a memo pad to write Japanese poems (*waka*).
kimono	long robe with wide sleeves worn tied with a sash
kokeshi	simple wooden dolls made in Japan
kuhi	haiku carved into a slab of stone
matcha	finely powdered green tea
niwaki	garden trees, often highly sculpted
obi	a sash worn over a kimono that can be tied in many shapes such as a drum or butterfly
sakura	cherry blossoms
shoji	a door or partition made of a wooden frame covered in rice paper
tanka	a Japanese poem form with five lines following the syllable count 5-7-5-7-7
tome ishi	stop stone. Stone tied with black twine to show that a path is temporarily closed, or a host's desire to show you the correct path.

Acknowledgments

I am thankful to The Richard & Helen DeVos Japanese Garden at Frederik Meijer Gardens & Sculpture Park. This esthetically curated gem of a garden provides meandering paths around a pond and tranquil views that lend itself to writing poetry.

I am grateful to LowellArts for choosing "Japanese Garden: Four Seasons," a poetry and art installation with artist Nola Nielsen, as a winner in their *WordView: Art Inspiring Art* juried exhibition of visual and literary artwork in 2022. The poems included were "Misaki Lantern," "gold midst cedar leaves," "Little cypress boat," and "Over the North Waterfall."

Thank you to George, Matthew, Hannah, Calvin, Shannon, and everyone at Wipf and Stock Publishers. Thank you to my book's endorsers, who've also been teachers and mentors to me. My thanks go out to Jane Wheeler and Andy Saur who were the first to critique these poems. I'm thankful for the creative Nola who so winsomely interpreted four poems into visual art. Thank you to Sharon Oleniczak for all your work and encouragement. My thanks to my dear friends and poets Kornelia Neele, Michal Frenzel, Amy Nemecek, and Denise Vredevoogd for reading these poems, giving input, and cheering me on. Thank you especially, Amy, for your excellent editorial work. Thank you to Shinji Yasugi and Yong Yasugi for reading with culturally sensitive eyes. Thank you to Claudia Chang for your encouraging chats about kanji. Thank you to Becky Adomaitis for your help with imaging the seasons' kanji.

And finally, thank you to my dear husband, Jim, my alpha reader who is always generous with praise and encouragement. Thank you for walking these paths with me.

About the Poet

Nellie deVries discovered the delight of right-brain creativity while writing poetry over a decade ago. Her work is featured in print and online journals and anthologies such as *Exhale*, *Peninsula Poets*, *Heart of Flesh*, and *Michigan Roots*. Her career was in the left-brain science of nursing, which she enjoyed for forty-five years before retiring. Nellie enjoys biking, hiking, and spending time with family in Michigan.